down syndrome
issues & information

Reading and writing

Reading and writing for infants with Down syndrome (0-5 years)

Gillian Bird and Sue Buckley

Summary – Teaching reading to teach talking is probably the single most effective intervention for helping children with Down syndrome to overcome their learning difficulties. Reading and writing skills are important for everyday life and for access to the world of literature for all children. They are also powerful tools for teaching speech and language to children with Down syndrome and for mediating their cognitive development. Beginning early, by introducing young children to reading from two years of age, will promote the development of both their spoken language and their literacy skills. This module explains how to teach reading to teach language and how language and literacy teaching can work together to promote the development of children with Down syndrome, beginning in the preschool years. Guidance on teaching methods and examples of activities show parents and teachers how to introduce young children to reading and other literacy activities. This module is linked with *Reading and writing development for individuals with Down syndrome - An overview*, which should be read first, to provider the reader with evidence for the benefits of early reading and the rationale behind the programme.

Series Editors

Sue Buckley and Gillian Bird

DSii-07-02-(en-gb) (January, 2001)

http://www.down-syndrome.org/information/

First published: January, 2001

Revision: 1.03; 2009

ISBN: 978-1-903806-10-4

A publication of Down Syndrome Education International

The Sarah Duffen Centre, Belmont Street, Southsea,
Hampshire, PO5 1NA, United Kingdom.

Telephone	+44 (0)23 9285 5330
Facsimile	+44 (0)23 9285 5320
E-mail	enquiries@downsed.org
Web Site	http://www.downsed.org/

Down Syndrome Education International is a charity, registered in England and Wales (number 1062823).

Typeset, printed and distributed by a subsidiary of Down Syndrome Education International:

Down Syndrome Education Enterprises Limited
The Sarah Duffen Centre, Belmont Street,
Southsea, Hampshire, PO5 1NA.
United Kingdom.

Contents

Authors

Gillian Bird

Director of Education and Information, Down Syndrome Education International, UK.

Sue Buckley

Emeritus Professor of Developmental Disability, Psychology Department, University of Portsmouth, UK
Director of Science and Research, Down Syndrome Education International, UK.

Acknowledgements

The authors would like to acknowledge the invaluable contribution of Leslie, Dilys and Sarah Duffen to their understanding of the importance of early reading for children with Down syndrome. Leslie's insights into the learning difficulties of children with Down syndrome drew the authors' attention to the issues and prompted their first research project in 1980.

The authors would also like to thank the children, parents, preschool and home teachers and psychologists that they have worked with across the UK and internationally, whose experience and knowledge have contributed to the content of this module.

Terminology

The term 'learning difficulty' is used throughout this book as it is the term currently in common use in the United Kingdom. The terms 'mental retardation', 'intellectual impairment' and 'developmental disability' are equivalent terms, used in other parts of the world.

Reading and writing for infants with Down syndrome (0-5 years)

Introduction

The importance of early reading for all children with Down syndrome

Reading activities may be the single most important intervention for promoting the speech, language and cognitive development of preschool children with Down syndrome. Leslie Duffen first drew the benefits and effectiveness of *teaching reading to teach talking* to our attention in 1979.[1-3] Leslie had introduced his daughter, Sarah, to reading at 3 years of age and observed that she could learn and use words that she had seen in print much more easily than words she only heard.

Since that time, we have taught many children with Down syndrome to read from 2 years of age and we are quite convinced that it is the single most effective way to help children overcome the learning difficulties associated with Down syndrome. All the early readers we know have made exceptional progress through school and into teenage life. All these children have been taught reading and language side by side by their parents in their preschool years. It is not difficult to teach children with Down syndrome language through reading, and most children would succeed and benefit if those around them had confidence in the value of reading and worked consistently in small steps.

Case studies, illustrating the progress of some of these children, and our research studies of reading, are discussed in detail in *Reading and writing development for individuals with Down syndrome - An overview.* We hope that all parents, home teachers, nursery and preschool teachers will use reading activities to help their children from the stage when they understand 50 words and are beginning to link two words together. We also hope that teaching reading will quickly be seen as an easy activity to plan and to develop, with parents and practitioners always working together.

We encourage record keeping and we are keen to collect information and as large a sample of early readers as we can to expand our knowledge of the short and long term benefits. If you are prepared to keep records of your child's progress and interested in joining a research study, please contact Down Syndrome Education International. We will provide regular feedback and advice to those who wish to take part in the study.

Why reading helps

Reading accelerates spoken language progress

Children with Down syndrome of all ages are usually able to learn more effectively from what they can see than from what they hear. Therefore, children will understand and remember how to say words and sentences earlier if they learn to read from a young age.

The progress of children varies

Some young children learn to read words and understand their meanings readily, even if they are unable to say them, and their reading skills go forward at a rapid rate. Most young children with Down syndrome can remember words if they are taught them, and even a small *sight* vocabulary (a reading vocabulary of words learned as whole words) helps them to develop language and reading skills in preparation for school. A small number of children find it difficult to remember words even with structured teaching, but can still gain from the language activities and games that are used to teach reading, especially if the activities are supported by pictures.

Some children will first need help to learn the basic skills used for learning how to read, for example; how to watch, listen, match and select, and they require positive teaching methods to successfully learn these skills. Once they have them, these skills will be used for learning across the curriculum for many years.

Early reading accelerates reading progress in school

Most children with Down syndrome will learn to read at school, even if they have not started earlier, but introducing reading at an earlier stage is likely to accelerate their progress, even if the child can only read one or two words when he or she commences school. Showing that children have already begun to learn to read and enjoy this activity may prevent unnecessary delays in teaching reading at school, especially if teachers are waiting for signs of 'reading readiness', as such signs do not apply to children with Down syndrome.

Children benefit from reading even when they cannot read by themselves

This module focuses on how to teach young children with Down syndrome to read, to help them to develop their spoken language skills and their independent literacy skills in later years. However, the authors also wish to stress that being involved in the literate community is the right of every child and does not depend on being able to read or write independently. Many of the benefits for knowledge and for language learning that come from being able to read can be gained from being read to every day. This should include the daily reading of storybooks to children. It should also include the making of individual books and topic books.

See also:
- *Reading and writing for individuals with Down syndrome – An overview*

The benefits of teaching reading to teach talking
- Children with Down syndrome have difficulty in learning their first language from listening
- They find learning visually easier than learning from listening
- Printed words seem to be easier for them to remember than spoken words
- Print can be used from as early as two years of age to support language learning
- Many children with Down syndrome can begin to learn to read from this early age and are able to remember printed words with ease
- All language targets can be taught with the aid of written material, even to children who are not able to remember the words and read independently
- Reading activities, at home and in the classroom, teach new vocabulary and grammar.
- Reading enables the child with Down syndrome to practise complete sentences - teaching grammar and supporting correct production
- Reading can help speech at the level of sounds (phonemes), whole word production and sentence production
- Reading to children with Down syndrome and teaching them to read, may be the most effective therapy for developing their speech and language skills from infancy right through school years
- Research studies show that reading instruction in school has a significant effect on language and working memory development for children with Down syndrome

Parents are the most effective teachers

For the majority of children with Down syndrome, as for other children, parents play a major role in developing early and later reading success, by providing enjoyable experiences with books and by playing reading games, as well as specifically teaching their child. Enjoyment and familiarity with books and reading games at home will give children confidence to continue to develop their reading skills when they start school.

Principles for learning

Encourage a love of books

Children will be much better prepared to learn to read if they have had plenty of experience of enjoying books. They will know that books are full of exciting and fun ideas, pictures and stories. They will also have seen print, and if the person reading with them has drawn their attention to the words as they read, children will realise the person that is reading is using the words on the page to tell the story. It is important to continue to read stories to children at home and at school, from the first year of life up to teenage years and beyond, especially to children who cannot read for pleasure by themselves. Unfortunately, when children are delayed, they may be read to less often than other children of their age group, when they could benefit from being read to more often. It is important to support their understanding and enjoyment of the text - by explaining the story and helping them to join in the reading activity. The repetition involved in reading favourite stories, until the child has learned them, is particularly valuable in teaching language and enables the child to join in.

Reading for meaning

Teach whole words and reading for meaning first

It is important to teach whole words and to develop *reading for meaning* as the first step - learning letter sounds will come later. All children learn a visual 'sight' vocabulary of words remembered and recognised as whole words, as they start to read, and slowly develop the phonic skills, which allow them to read unfamiliar words and to spell.

We all read to understand the messages in the text. We want beginning readers to be able to understand words and simple sentences in books before drawing their attention to the link between letters on the page and sounds in words (phonics). A child should have a sight vocabulary of at least 50 words, which he or she can read with confidence, in different sentences, with understanding, before teaching any phonics.

Teaching phonics

The words that the child can already read with confidence can then be used to teach him/her letter sound links by putting together several of the child's own 'sight' words which rhyme or which start or end with the same letter and sound. It is easy for the child to begin to understand the letter/sound links in this way as he/she can already say the words. In our experience, children who are being taught to read as a language teaching activity, soon begin to see the regularities in words for themselves. For example, they see the difference between 'dog' and 'dogs', boy' and 'boys' or 'run' and 'running', 'jump' and 'jumping' - sometimes before they are four years old.

For most children (with or without Down syndrome) phonics, which are most useful for writing and spelling rather than reading, are learned most effectively during writing and spelling activities.

Over time, children with Down syndrome learn to read in the same way as other children. They proceed through the same stages as other children in first establishing a sight vocabulary (logographic reading) and then being able to use phonic knowledge to spell and to decode words (alphabetic reading) but they rely on logographic strategies to read for longer (that is at higher reading levels) than other children.

Many children with Down syndrome between the ages of 4 and 5 years, who have received reading instruction from a young age, will have a sight vocabulary, will be able to read words in sentences, will be able to make short sentences from the words they can read, to read 'home-made books' to others, and will know letter names and sounds (although they may not be able to say all of these) when they commence school. Therefore, most children with Down syndrome will still be logographic readers at five though some may understand and make use of letter sounds, and so are becoming alphabetic readers.

Develop writing alongside early reading

Most children with Down syndrome of 4 to 5 years are not able to write words, but are learning to hold and use pens and crayons for writing, colouring, painting, tracing and drawing activities. Some children are able to draw, colour, trace over large letters and numbers and may be able to write some or all of the letters in their name or from the alphabet. However, the delayed handwriting development of the majority of children with Down syndrome should not delay the introduction of reading, writing and drawing activities. These can be supported using alternatives to writing such as sponge, plastic or magnetic letters, a white board, a computer, letter and word cards. It is important that children are encouraged in the development of their fine and gross motor skills with equipment and multi-sensory materials, and that they are helped to be successful with the equipment provided.

Use positive teaching and make it fun

As with all teaching activities, it is important to make learning enjoyable and successful by planning appropriate activities for the individual child and by supporting success by taking turns at the activity with your child, by modelling correct responses, by prompting the child to succeed and by creating an atmosphere of fun. Remember that repetition and correct practice are the keys to successful learning and that the main difference between faster and slower learners is that slower learners need more practice and praise. Do not assume that the slower learner cannot learn and give up too soon. In addition to teaching a planned sight vocabulary in small steps, make simple books for language teaching and read them with your child, put names on items at home and at school, wear name badges, play games with words and you will find that your child will progress.

The world is full of print, and as early as 1969, workers in an institution in the USA[4] observed that a group of children with Down syndrome could learn to read, when they realized that the children had all learned to read their names spontaneously by seeing them on chairs and coat pegs. Almost all children with Down syndrome are capable of reaching a level of reading

See also:

• *Reading and writing development for individuals with Down syndrome - An overview*

See also:

• *Motor skills development for infants with Down syndrome - An overview*

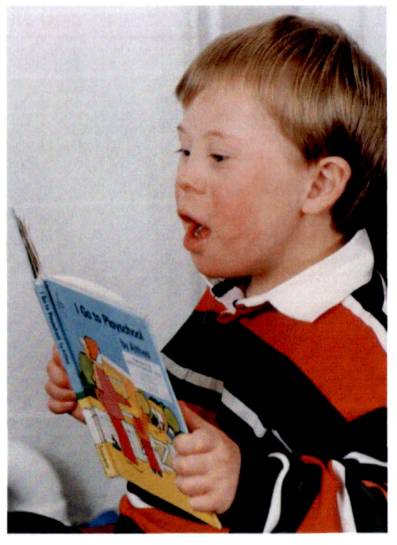

achievement that will be functionally useful if we, their parents and teachers, believe that this is possible and steadily help them to progress.

Teaching reading

The links between reading and spoken language

Activities at each child's comprehension level

> **Reading is a language activity**
>
> • Choose words and sentences for reading activities at the child's language level
> • The meanings of new words and grammar can be taught by reading

When introducing reading instruction to children with Down syndrome, the links between reading and spoken language need to be thought of at all stages. Children can only read with understanding if they already know and understand the words, the grammar and the sentence structures used in the text. Therefore it is important to introduce reading activities at each child's language comprehension level. Children with Down syndrome will almost always be delayed in language comprehension compared with other children of the same age and it is important to begin with vocabulary that they understand and with short simple sentence structures.

As children with Down syndrome progress and begin to read simple text with confidence, using language that they already know, reading then becomes a powerful tool to use to teach new vocabulary and grammar. It is possible to follow the simple rule below to be sure that the language level of 'home-made' reading activities is appropriate.

Expand the child's speech to create written sentences

Listen to the child and once they can communicate, take the child's own words and make the shortest correct sentence for them. For example, if the child says "sand" or "play sand" when asked "What did you do today?" write 'I played in the sand'. The reader will notice that this is the way we help children to develop their spoken language. It is an example of expansion – the term used when we speak to young children and expand their one and two word utterances.

If this simple rule is followed, the language used in literacy activities will be at the level of the child's language comprehension and it will help the child to learn the grammar of and to say longer sentences. This module should be used in parallel with *Speech and language development for infants with Down syndrome (0-5 years)*, as the words and sentences used in reading activities should be chosen from the same ones that are being used in the speech and language activities. Start with teaching your child to read words that you know he/she already understands and then introduce new ones in order to use reading activities to teach comprehension of new words and grammar, once your child is showing that he/she can read with understanding.

The importance of active involvement of the child

If a child is going to enjoy learning to read, and if reading activities are going to help speech and language development, the child must be *actively involved* in the whole activity, not just passively reading or copying work prepared for him/her. This is not always easy to achieve and clearly younger children may need more help to decide on words and ideas to record than older children, but it is a very important principle. Children should be encouraged to choose what they want to record by discussing the activity with them. Use flashcards and encourage the child to choose the key words and then to build the sentence. Active thinking and engagement in the task is necessary for learning.

Resources

Children may need a variety of resources for teaching and learning - to help motivate them. Some resources can be bought, especially colourful vocabulary teaching books and picture dictionaries. However, the materials for structured teaching are likely to be created at home. These may include:

* word cards, (bought, home-made, hand written or printed from a computer, on card or thick paper
* home-made books and games, such as matching games, 'lift the flap' books, 'fishing' games, 'posting' games and 'finding' or 'shopping' games
* photographs and pictures
* published reading books, vocabulary and topic books
* early phonic activities and schemes to learn about letter sounds and names

Teaching methods

Children with Down syndrome learn to read in the same way as all other children but they may need smaller steps, more practice and more structured guidance to achieve success. Teaching methods will include:

* matching games of various types, matching words to pictures and objects, posting boxes and sorting games
* selecting games (e.g. 'give me the word for ...?', 'where's the ...?', 'let's find....', 'show me...?'
* graded practice with independent reading, for example, finding and saying the last word of a familiar sentence or reading known words using word cards, sentence cards, or pointing or selecting words using the computer
* modelled reading so that the child imitates single words and words in a sentence, with encouragement to look and point at each word and enjoy the game
* offering limited choices to help children choose words correctly
* 'naming' games when you are sure that your child can read words successfully (see page 8)

It is very important that materials and games motivate the child. There are many activities, methods and games that parents can create and use including:

* 'lift the flap' books (read the word and see the picture underneath), or just to lift the flap and see the word underneath and read it
* picture and word books, posting, fishing, sticking, hiding and finding games, shopping games
* action games where the word (verb) or sentence with a verb in, is read and then the action undertaken
* games which involve taking turns with the family, playing in a small group or with a pair of children

- personal books with photographs of family, friends or tailored to the child's particular interests,

- adapted materials, such as words stuck under or on top of pieces of inset puzzle, or words stuck on top of puzzle pieces and pictures underneath

- always use positive approaches that support and help to achieve success.

Remember that learning from listening is difficult for children with Down syndrome and that their strength is in visual learning. Therefore, reading success will be achieved by 'look and say' methods and games which teach a sight vocabulary.

Hearing loss

The incidence of mild to moderate hearing loss in children with Down syndrome is high and remembering some simple guidelines can help to compensate for their difficulties. Many children may only have a small amount of hearing loss, although hearing levels can fluctuate, but even a small amount of hearing loss affects listening and can affect behaviour, performance and language learning. Reading and phonic work requires good auditory discrimination. Therefore, for all children with Down syndrome it is advisable to take account of possible hearing difficulties at all times by gaining children's full attention and working in environments that do not have competing background noise.

Teaching words and early reading skills

Video tapes, explaining the rational for reading and showing children with Down syndrome illustrating the reading activities and methods, are available from Down Syndrome Education International[5-8].

How to choose words and teach them

The choice of words for any child will depend on the stage the child has reached in learning language, the child's age, cultural and family background, the child's interests and things he or she likes to communicate about, and the curriculum the child is learning from. This section describes recommendations for beginning to teach reading using whole words and how to extend vocabulary and grammar for young children, aged approximately 2 to 5 years.

Begin with words that children understand

Reading activities can be introduced when a child understands 50 to 100 spoken words and can match and select pictures, that is, play a picture lotto game and demonstrate comprehension of words. The same method will be used to teach sight words.

Children who have 50 to 100 single words (signed or spoken) in their expressive vocabularies and are developing two word comprehension should learn to read words *that they already understand*. These are likely to be very young children with Down syndrome (aged 30 to 42 months) but some children will be school age when they reach a 100-word stage and two-word comprehension.

First reading activities should be used to teach them how to link two words and ideas together, therefore the first words chosen for reading should be words to make two word phrases such as 'more dinner', 'Daddy gone.' Prac-

---

Teaching reading - Key principles

- Teach whole words first (phonics later)
- Start with words that the child already understands
- Choose words to build short sentences
- Focus on reading for meaning from the outset
- Develop writing skills alongside reading skills
- Teach new vocabulary and grammar through print, once reading is progressing

---

tising reading two words together often helps the child to start saying two words together.

The record sheets at the end of the module allow you to record reading progress and to observe the transfer from reading to speaking for your child.

How to teach matching, selecting and naming

Matching single words:

- Make 2 identical flashcards for each of 4 words.

- Put one word in front of your child; give the duplicate word to the child and say: "This says (cup/shoe...). Put it with the one that is the same".

- Guide the child to complete the task successfully, i.e. physically guide his or her hands, prompt and praise.

- Match a photo to the word, or turn a word card over to show the corresponding picture, to aid understanding that the written word means the same as the spoken word illustrated by the photo.

- Matching games can include lotto, fishing, posting boxes, find the word in the room or on the picture (for younger children), and snap or other competitive 'board' games for word matching (for older children) to add variety and maintain interest.

- Some children can remember words by being shown them and told them, especially as reading skills develop, and do not need to match words in this structured way.

- Matching encourages the child to look carefully at the word and to realise how it looks the same or different compared with other words. Children will learn more accurate discrimination through matching, and in later stages of reading may need to go back to matching to emphasise and learn differences between words with similar looks or meanings e.g. 'is', 'in', 'it', 'the', 'this'.

Selecting: learning to associate the name with the word

- Use flashcards that the child has learned to match; lay 2 or 3 in front of the child and say: "Give me (or show me) the word (cup/shoe...)"

- Guide the child through the correct response; when he or she can select 2 words, add a third - slowly build up the number of words to choose from.

Naming

- Children may name words using signs or spoken words.

- Articulation problems may mean that spoken words are not clear. Praise and encourage approximations to word-reading as practice helps children to make their speech clearer.

- Show the child the word and say: "What is this? It's a (cup/shoe...) Can you say cup?"

- Encourage children to imitate words.

- Repeat words (or whole sentences) after they have signed or said them, to help pronunciation.

> **Recommended order for matching**
>
> - Picture to picture
> - Word to word (matching, naming and selecting)
> - Word to picture (comprehension game, adds interest, demonstrates reading ability and understanding)

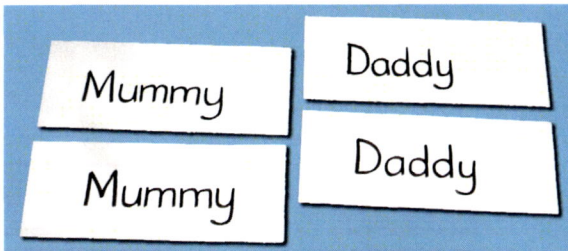

Figure 1a. Word matching using flashcards

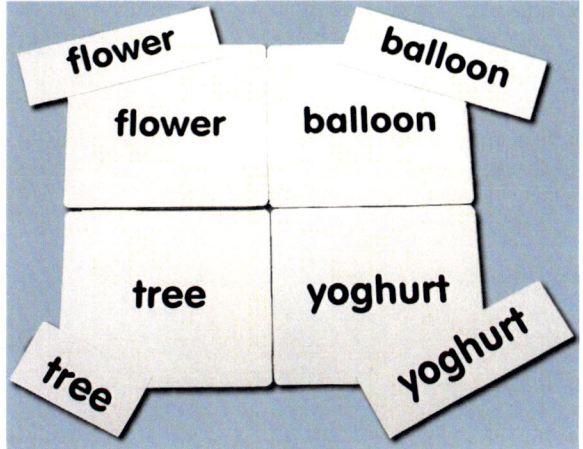

Figure 1b. Word matching using flashcards

Figure 2. Word and picture matching for reading comprehension using flashcards and picture cards

- Use errorless techniques by prompting children with the correct answer, until they can say the word, without hesitation.

Which words?

Words for reading can be chosen from children's own vocabulary comprehension list, assessed by using the word lists provided in the *DownsEd Vocabulary Checklists*. All children are likely to begin to learn to read with some of the words from the first 120 words checklist, particularly 'Mummy', 'Daddy', child's name, brothers and sisters names, important people or pets names (Figure 1). They are then more likely to be interested in reading games about words for their favourite animals (e.g. cat, dog, cow, horse), favourite food and drink (e.g. banana, apple, juice, yoghurt), favourite toys and familiar objects (e.g. car, keys, book, ball, bag), favourite real or play activities (e.g. play, eats, drinks, runs, sleeps, like(s), dances, gone, up, down), social words (e.g. bye bye, yes, no, there, please) and favourite places (e.g. park, beach, farm, garden, shop, swimming pool) Colour words and 'big' and 'little' can also be taught, as these can also be used to teach children to join words together in speech and sign. Reading colour, shape and size words often seems to help children to understand them.

Children need only learn a small sight vocabulary to begin to join words together meaningfully and usefully. Choose 4 or 5 nouns and a few adjectives and verbs to make up their first 8-10 words, so that you can build short phrases and sentences and make individual books right away.

The *DownsEd Language Cards*[9] illustrated in Figures 1 and 2 can be used and provide pictures for many words from the first vocabulary checklist. Matching words to pictures enables children to demonstrate that they can read them with understanding as some of the successful readers may not at first be able say the words, although they may sign them.

Take photographs of toys, objects, people and activities that are important in children's daily routines to make personal materials. Introduce reading using matching, selecting and naming games, described above. Begin with picture matching and when the child can match and select pictures proceed to word matching (word to word without the picture) and to matching the word to the picture. It may be helpful to use a record sheet in the early stages of learning to read, to keep track of new words introduced, and when the child was able to match, select and name them. This will also be useful for the revision of old words, as well as learning new ones. If children find it very difficult to remember particular words after a lot of successful matching, try new words that may hold more interest for them or be visually easier for them to remember. Words that are very different in size and outline shape are likely to help beginners to succeed, such as 'cat' and 'aeroplane', or 'dog' and 'banana'.

If children are not at all interested in learning to read words using the games suggested, leave it and try again at a later date, with lots of encouragement for matching. Give them practice at picture matching games, which are fun and will also teach the attention skills and habits they will benefit from when they begin to learn to read words. Keep reading books to them and try not to let your anxiety show if progress is slow. Keep reading games short and end them on a successful note, use turn taking (my turn, your turn) and *ask* them if they would like to do the words again. Make the materials associated with the reading game interesting, for example by using a decorated folder or box for their words which is clearly their own and only comes out when they are reading. Let them show others their folder or word box or homemade book with pride, and praise them. Some children will want to read to others, some just enjoy other people reading them, until they feel confident or able to read themselves.

Figure 3. Example of using a 'carrier' phrase, 'I like'

Figure 4. Example of simple sentence activity

Make short phrases and simple sentences from the words the child can read

Make simple books with short sentences, using the child's sight vocabulary. Introduce the simple phrases and sentences that you want your child to use in speech as early as possible during your teaching activities. The DownsEd Sentences and Grammar Checklist will help you to choose short phrases that your child is likely to soon begin to say or sign: learning to read will help them to do this more quickly.

For example, for children not yet joining **two words** together, but who can read some of the word suggested above, teach **possessives**, such as 'Mummy's/Daddy's car', 'Daddy's bag', 'Daddy's keys'.

Or add colour and other **attribute** words, such as 'red ball', 'yellow car' etc.

To help children to join three words together in their speech, make three word phrases with words they can read, for example, 'Sarah likes banana', 'Mummy likes apple', 'Sam drinks juice', 'Douglas eats yoghurt'. Four family names (Mummy, Daddy, child's name and one other), four food types and one verb such as 'eats' or 'gone' will generate 16 different 3-word phrases. Adding one more verb, for example, 'likes' will make another 16 phrases. The authors think it is valuable to practice two and three word phrases with a small set of well-learned *sight* words, for example, 6 or 8 *sight* words that can be combined, before introducing too many different sentence types and new words (Figures 3/4). When children can read sentences with words they know well, they are likely to find it easier to learn other new words and sentence types, building on their success, and developing their reading skills with confidence.

When children are confident in reading their sight vocabulary, then many different 3 word phrases can be made using the words they can read, for example, 'Daddy's big bike', 'Mummy's brown shoes', 'the cat sleeps', 'the dog sleeps', 'the cat plays', 'the horse runs'. Adding some words like 'this', 'here', 'is', my', 'look', 'at', 'the', 'I' and 'and' will lead easily into many more 3 and 4 word phrases using this same sight vocabulary, for example, 'my big red ball', 'this is my house', 'look at the horse', 'mummy and daddy', 'I like playing ball'.

New vocabulary can be added from the checklists, depending upon the child's interests and comprehension, for example, number words 'one', 'two' and 'three', increasing the range of animal words, other nouns and verbs. These will be introduced naturally by making topic books (see below) based on everyday life events and interests, with new words on flashcards and in sentences.

When children reach this stage, they are likely to move easily into published reading books with a core vocabulary. However, published books probably will not replace the need for home-made books and topic books, unless the picture content and sentences are within or near to the child's language understanding. Topic and personal books will continue to remain an extremely beneficial teaching tool alongside other reading books well into children's infant school years.

Make topic and personal books

Topic books can be made using photo albums or scrapbooks with words, sentences and pictures, using children's interests as a guide. These will help to teach new words in *categories*, for example, the rooms of a house, animal words, garden words, clothes words, transport words and action words (verbs) and help the child to practice saying old or well learned words in a wide range of sentence types. This will teach new grammar and aid spoken language. By creating books about family members and pets, children will find names that are both interesting and easy to read. Books about real activities that have happened, such as visits, outings or regular occurrences are usually interesting for children to read and to talk about. A camera to photograph and help parents to record important events, people and places with accompanying written language is a tremendous asset for this purpose. As advised in other sections, remember to use the "small" words of speech, such as, 'the', 'at', 'in', 'is', 'his/her' and 'she/he' in sentences. (These are the closed class grammar or function words that the children find difficult to master). Help the children to be successful with these words if they find them difficult to remember by prompting them and by using a similar type of sentence type, or 'frame' in each book, so that they have lots of repetition of reading these words along with the well established sight vocabulary they can remember more easily (Figure 5).

Children who understand two or more ideas and words linked together, but who are not yet able to say two or three together, will benefit from reading words in two and three word phrases. This will help them to use phrases in sign and speech.

Some computer software also has short phrases built into the software for very young children, for example, *Speaking for Myself*.[10]

Social and communicative language, early questions forms, negatives, prepositions and the present tense can be taught and practised by making books that contain short phrases, for example, 'What's that?' (a book/a cat/a tree), 'Who's that?' (Me/Mummy/Jamie), 'Where is it?' (in the box/on the chair/under the bed), 'I like (yoghurt/coke/crisps'), 'I can (jump/run/sit/sleep), 'Mum/Dad/Penny.. (can jump), 'I want (the pens, the book, a drink)', books to teach plurals and negatives e.g. using 'no ', or 'not' in a sentence . Books can be illustrated with stick figures as well as photos – these do not need to be elaborate (see Figure 6). Children should

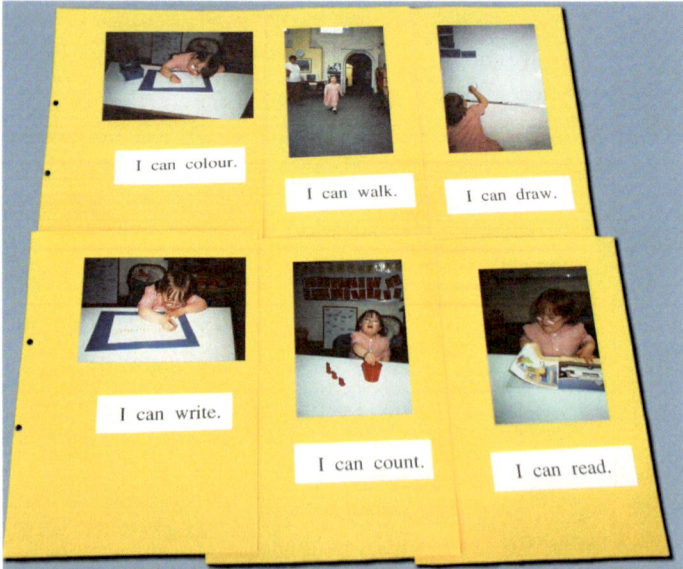

Figure 5. An individual book using a 'sentence frame'

Figure 6. 'Home-made' reading boards

then progress to reading simple, grammatically correct sentences of varying length, even though these will contain some words they cannot yet read independently. Build sentences from the language used with and around children, much as they would hear it spoken.

Many illustrated examples of these types of personalised materials can be found in Jane Beadman's book, *Including All*.[11]

Computer software is particularly good for teaching language with reading, and can be better than picture materials as the action of verbs can be shown by moving pictures on the screen, so that people can be seen to be, for example, be 'eating' or 'dancing'.

In the USA, materials to teach reading and language to young preschool children at home have been developed by the parents of a child with Down syndrome, Sue and Jo Kotlinski.[12] These 'Love and Learning' materials include video and audiotapes and books and they have received positive reviews from parents and professionals in the USA.[13,14]

Remember that all children progress at different rates and that all reading is valuable and an achievement to celebrate. The range of reading vocabulary learned by children with Down syndrome at the age of 4 years may vary between 1 or 2 words up to 400 words or even more.

Early writing skills alongside reading

When children can read words in a sentence, they can also 'write' the sentence, by ordering the words on flashcards. To begin with, this will be by copying sentences they have been taught, or short sentences they have memorised from their reading books. They can match whole or parts of a sentence to the whole sentence, or choose the last word to place at the end of a sentence (Figure 6).

Children can be helped to learn writing and language skills by using a memory training kit. This could be a 'lift the flap' chart like that shown in Figure 7. Not only can they read the words in the sentence by lifting each flap, they can also lift the first flap, say the word, close the flap and say it again, then lift the first and second flaps, close and say, then lift the first, second and third flaps, close and say, and so on, in order to memorise the sentence structure.

They can lift and read the words under the first and second flaps and 'guess' what is under the third flap. After reading the entire sentence and then closing the flaps, they can go from the beginning of the sentence, checking each word by lifting the flap after they have said or guessed it.

'Lift the flap' charts can be used for many early language, memory, reading and writing games. They can be helpful for learning any sequence of

Figure 7. 'Lift the flap' charts

activities using picture materials, as well as the emphasis given to learning to read in this module.

For reading games and writing, we recommend that the charts are personalized and decorated, but not on the cards that show words, as pictures may slow down the process of learning to read words and sentences. Once a sentence has been read, it is then appropriate to turn another flap to look at a picture that illustrates the meaning of the whole sentence.

Using reading to teach language

Children will have learned about language and how it is used, and will have practised words and sentences by speaking or expressing themselves in sign by doing the reading activities in the sections above. If they have experienced success with reading and enjoyed reading, sharing and showing home-made books and sentences, reading can take them even further by teaching words and sentences that they do not yet understand. Reading a sentence will help them to remember and process the words in the sentence and to talk about the sentence: undertaking real and pretend play activities and using pictures in their books will teach them to understand new structures.

Children with Down syndrome, who begin to read early, are likely to reach the point where they can and should read sentences that are beyond their current understanding of spoken language. This will help them to develop new language skills through visual, written language and bypass their difficulties with learning language from listening to spoken language (see *Reading and writing for individuals with Down syndrome - An overview*).

Learning about letters and sounds

Young children with Down syndrome learn to read by remembering whole words and their meanings before they are able to separate out the sounds in words and apply their letter sound knowledge to the task of reading and writing. This is consistent with what we know about the children's speech, language and cognitive development in their early years. They are, however, able to learn about letters, the sounds associated with the letters and their names, and this ability can be used to help their speech perception, production and literacy skills in primary school. Therefore, young children with Down syndrome should have access to and enjoy typical pre-school learning games about the letters and sounds of their language, and success in this area can be used explicitly to help them to speak more clearly.

Learning about letters will help them in school, where they will continue to participate in phonic teaching activities with their peers. Meanwhile, their sight vocabulary for reading whole words will be increasing and at a later stage in their reading than is usual for typically developing peers, they will be able to use their phonic skills for reading and writing.

Children will learn how to 'hear' and 'see' the letters within words, beginning with short phonically regular words of two and three letters. Working with rhyming sets of words helps to simplify the task.

Children with Down syndrome can be enabled to participate in this type of work by allowing them to show their choices physically rather than verbally. Letter cards, let-

Figure 8. Example of letter/sound game

ters that can be handled, or pointing to select letters from a short list, will all make this easier for them (Figure 8).

Finger spelling may help some children remember letters and letter patterns and learning to finger spell can be an enjoyable game for a group of children to learn together.

Children who develop handwriting skills early may be able to write letters as they participate in phonic teaching games and activities, although most young children in the infant age range will need to use letters on card, made of sponge or plastic, or letter magnets. Suitable computer software will also help them to learn. Children with Down syndrome can be explicitly taught to read, write and say sounds together to develop their speech production alongside reading and writing skills.

Visually supported reading and writing using pictures and symbols

Most children with Down syndrome are able to learn to read using ordinary text from the beginning and the authors' actively discourage the use of symbols to teach reading unless a child is making no progress at all with reading print. Symbols are all around us in the environment and they can enhance learning and support our understanding in many ways, but using symbols for reading words and sentences if they are not necessary is confusing to the child and introduces another symbolic system he or she does not need.

However, for children who practice often but still seem to find it difficult to select or remember words, pictures and picture symbols can add to the fun and success of reading. These can be taught in the same way as teaching written words, with matching games initially, and combinations of words, symbols and pictures can be used together. Working with symbols is different from working with words, and symbols do not necessarily map onto words in a sentence. Symbols can support understanding of ideas represented in words (for example, question words) and sentences. Symbols can be added to pages or next to words and sentences, as can other visual aids and objects to help children understand and remember. As a general rule, introduction of picture symbols for children of preschool age is not necessary for learning to read written words, although the use of pictures or symbols may make recorded work and activities more interesting and aid comprehension by illustrating concepts.

Conclusions

This module has emphasised the value of teaching reading and using reading activities to develop the spoken language skills of children with Down syndrome – a *teaching reading to teach talking* programme. Children are introduced to reading in a fun way, first learning to read whole words by playing matching, selecting and naming games and then moving on to reading short sentences and longer sentences in topic books. All the activities and reading should be based on the child's interests and experiences. All the reading activities must be linked to the child's language comprehension and language learning needs and this can be done using the DownsEd checklists. Children who have not made rapid progress with reading will still have benefited from these reading games and activities, as they are powerful and enjoyable ways of improved their understanding and use of spoken language.

We hope that it has provided enough guidance and practical ideas to enable you to teach your child to read and enjoy reading activities, and that these experiences will have prepared them to continue to succeed in developing their reading and writing in school. We are confident that if you have been able to use the ideas presented, you will have improved the spoken language skills of your child. Many of the ideas and activities discussed are explained and illustrated in the videotapes that we have published on reading and language,[5-8] and more valuable guidance and ideas for activities will be found in Patricia Oelwein's book, *Teaching reading to children with Down syndrome.*[15]

References

1. Duffen, L. (1974). *Teaching reading to teach talking*. Cheam, UK: Down's Babies Association, South East Branch.

2. Duffen, L. (1976). Teaching reading to children with little or no language. *Remedial Education*, 11, 139.

3. Duffen, L. (1979). For reading read listening. *Learning*, 1, 61-3.

4. Rhodes, L., Gooch, B., Siegelman, E. Y., Behrns, C. and Metzger, R. (1969). *A language stimulation and reading program for severely retarded mongoloid children*. California Mental Health Research Monograph, 11. State of California, Department of Mental Hygiene.

5. Down Syndrome Education International (1983). *Reading skills in pre-school children with Down syndrome*. (Video) Portsmouth, UK: Down Syndrome Education International.

6. Down Syndrome Education International (1986). *The development of language and reading skills in children with Down syndrome*. (Video) Portsmouth, UK: Down Syndrome Education International.

7. Down Syndrome Education International (1995). *Understanding Down syndrome (1) - Learning to talk*. (Video) Portsmouth, UK: Down Syndrome Education International.

8. Down Syndrome Education International (1995). *Understanding Down syndrome (2) - Learning to read*. (Video) Portsmouth, UK: Down Syndrome Education International.

9. The Down Syndrome Educational Trust. (1996). Language Cards. Portsmouth, UK: DownsEd.

10. Black, B. [Computer Software]. (1997). *Speaking for Myself*. Penryn, Cornwall, UK: Topoligika Software.

11. Beadman, J. (1999). *Including All*. Torquay, Devon, UK: Devon Learning Resources.

12. Kotlinski, S., and Kotlinski, J. (2000). Love and Learning Learning Kits. Dearborn, MI, USA: Love and Learning.

13. Dickinson, L. L. (October 15, 2000). The use of a reading program and signing to develop language and communication skills in a toddler with Down syndrome. Love and Learning Web Site. <http://www.loveandlearning.com/lauralee.shtml> (Accessed: October 15, 2000)

14. Kumin, L. (1997). Literacy and language. *Communicating Together*, 19.

15. Oelwein, P.L. (1995). *Teaching reading to children with Down syndrome : a guide for parents and teachers*. Bethesda, MD: Woodbine House.

Appendix I - Reading progress record sheet for new words

This sheet can be used if you wish to record your child's word reading progress and to observe the transfer of new words into his/her everyday spoken language.

Flashcard word	Matches	Selects	Names	Used in speech
_____	☐ __/__/__	☐ __/__/__	☐ __/__/__	☐ __/__/__
_____	☐ __/__/__	☐ __/__/__	☐ __/__/__	☐ __/__/__
_____	☐ __/__/__	☐ __/__/__	☐ __/__/__	☐ __/__/__
_____	☐ __/__/__	☐ __/__/__	☐ __/__/__	☐ __/__/__
_____	☐ __/__/__	☐ __/__/__	☐ __/__/__	☐ __/__/__
_____	☐ __/__/__	☐ __/__/__	☐ __/__/__	☐ __/__/__
_____	☐ __/__/__	☐ __/__/__	☐ __/__/__	☐ __/__/__
_____	☐ __/__/__	☐ __/__/__	☐ __/__/__	☐ __/__/__
_____	☐ __/__/__	☐ __/__/__	☐ __/__/__	☐ __/__/__
_____	☐ __/__/__	☐ __/__/__	☐ __/__/__	☐ __/__/__
_____	☐ __/__/__	☐ __/__/__	☐ __/__/__	☐ __/__/__
_____	☐ __/__/__	☐ __/__/__	☐ __/__/__	☐ __/__/__
_____	☐ __/__/__	☐ __/__/__	☐ __/__/__	☐ __/__/__
_____	☐ __/__/__	☐ __/__/__	☐ __/__/__	☐ __/__/__
_____	☐ __/__/__	☐ __/__/__	☐ __/__/__	☐ __/__/__
_____	☐ __/__/__	☐ __/__/__	☐ __/__/__	☐ __/__/__
_____	☐ __/__/__	☐ __/__/__	☐ __/__/__	☐ __/__/__
_____	☐ __/__/__	☐ __/__/__	☐ __/__/__	☐ __/__/__
_____	☐ __/__/__	☐ __/__/__	☐ __/__/__	☐ __/__/__
_____	☐ __/__/__	☐ __/__/__	☐ __/__/__	☐ __/__/__
_____	☐ __/__/__	☐ __/__/__	☐ __/__/__	☐ __/__/__
_____	☐ __/__/__	☐ __/__/__	☐ __/__/__	☐ __/__/__
_____	☐ __/__/__	☐ __/__/__	☐ __/__/__	☐ __/__/__
_____	☐ __/__/__	☐ __/__/__	☐ __/__/__	☐ __/__/__
_____	☐ __/__/__	☐ __/__/__	☐ __/__/__	☐ __/__/__
_____	☐ __/__/__	☐ __/__/__	☐ __/__/__	☐ __/__/__
_____	☐ __/__/__	☐ __/__/__	☐ __/__/__	☐ __/__/__
_____	☐ __/__/__	☐ __/__/__	☐ __/__/__	☐ __/__/__
_____	☐ __/__/__	☐ __/__/__	☐ __/__/__	☐ __/__/__
_____	☐ __/__/__	☐ __/__/__	☐ __/__/__	☐ __/__/__
_____	☐ __/__/__	☐ __/__/__	☐ __/__/__	☐ __/__/__
_____	☐ __/__/__	☐ __/__/__	☐ __/__/__	☐ __/__/__
_____	☐ __/__/__	☐ __/__/__	☐ __/__/__	☐ __/__/__
_____	☐ __/__/__	☐ __/__/__	☐ __/__/__	☐ __/__/__
_____	☐ __/__/__	☐ __/__/__	☐ __/__/__	☐ __/__/__
_____	☐ __/__/__	☐ __/__/__	☐ __/__/__	☐ __/__/__
_____	☐ __/__/__	☐ __/__/__	☐ __/__/__	☐ __/__/__
_____	☐ __/__/__	☐ __/__/__	☐ __/__/__	☐ __/__/__
_____	☐ __/__/__	☐ __/__/__	☐ __/__/__	☐ __/__/__
_____	☐ __/__/__	☐ __/__/__	☐ __/__/__	☐ __/__/__

Appendix 2 - Reading progress record sheet for phrases

This sheet can be used if you wish to record your child's progress with reading phrases and function words, and to observe the transfer of these new words/phrases into his/her everyday spoken language.

Phrases	Introduced	Can read	Used in spoken language
_____	☐ _/_/_	☐ _/_/_	☐ _/_/_
_____	☐ _/_/_	☐ _/_/_	☐ _/_/_
_____	☐ _/_/_	☐ _/_/_	☐ _/_/_
_____	☐ _/_/_	☐ _/_/_	☐ _/_/_
_____	☐ _/_/_	☐ _/_/_	☐ _/_/_
_____	☐ _/_/_	☐ _/_/_	☐ _/_/_
_____	☐ _/_/_	☐ _/_/_	☐ _/_/_
_____	☐ _/_/_	☐ _/_/_	☐ _/_/_
_____	☐ _/_/_	☐ _/_/_	☐ _/_/_
_____	☐ _/_/_	☐ _/_/_	☐ _/_/_
_____	☐ _/_/_	☐ _/_/_	☐ _/_/_
_____	☐ _/_/_	☐ _/_/_	☐ _/_/_
_____	☐ _/_/_	☐ _/_/_	☐ _/_/_
_____	☐ _/_/_	☐ _/_/_	☐ _/_/_
_____	☐ _/_/_	☐ _/_/_	☐ _/_/_
_____	☐ _/_/_	☐ _/_/_	☐ _/_/_
_____	☐ _/_/_	☐ _/_/_	☐ _/_/_
_____	☐ _/_/_	☐ _/_/_	☐ _/_/_
_____	☐ _/_/_	☐ _/_/_	☐ _/_/_
_____	☐ _/_/_	☐ _/_/_	☐ _/_/_
_____	☐ _/_/_	☐ _/_/_	☐ _/_/_
_____	☐ _/_/_	☐ _/_/_	☐ _/_/_
_____	☐ _/_/_	☐ _/_/_	☐ _/_/_
_____	☐ _/_/_	☐ _/_/_	☐ _/_/_
_____	☐ _/_/_	☐ _/_/_	☐ _/_/_
_____	☐ _/_/_	☐ _/_/_	☐ _/_/_
_____	☐ _/_/_	☐ _/_/_	☐ _/_/_
_____	☐ _/_/_	☐ _/_/_	☐ _/_/_
_____	☐ _/_/_	☐ _/_/_	☐ _/_/_
_____	☐ _/_/_	☐ _/_/_	☐ _/_/_
_____	☐ _/_/_	☐ _/_/_	☐ _/_/_
_____	☐ _/_/_	☐ _/_/_	☐ _/_/_
_____	☐ _/_/_	☐ _/_/_	☐ _/_/_
_____	☐ _/_/_	☐ _/_/_	☐ _/_/_
_____	☐ _/_/_	☐ _/_/_	☐ _/_/_
_____	☐ _/_/_	☐ _/_/_	☐ _/_/_
_____	☐ _/_/_	☐ _/_/_	☐ _/_/_
_____	☐ _/_/_	☐ _/_/_	☐ _/_/_
_____	☐ _/_/_	☐ _/_/_	☐ _/_/_
_____	☐ _/_/_	☐ _/_/_	☐ _/_/_